Where Is Liberia?

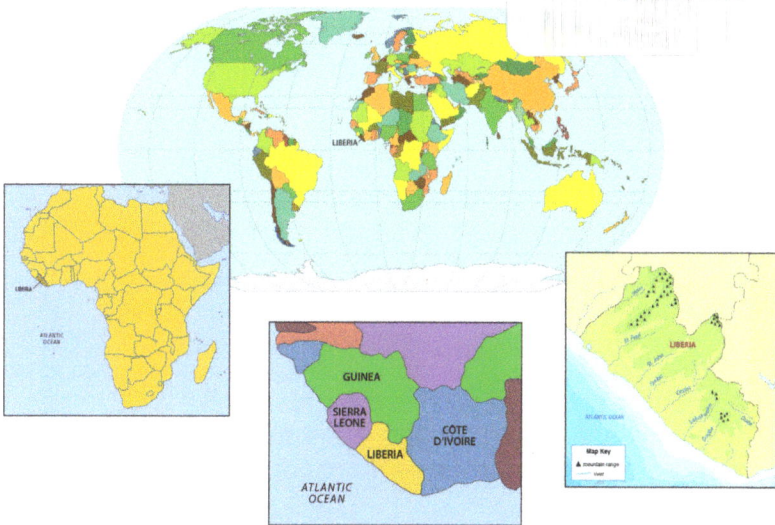

LIBERIA

GUINEA

SIERRA LEONE

LIBERIA

CÔTE D'IVOIRE

ATLANTIC OCEAN

By Nancy O'Leary

Library For All Ltd.

Where Is Liberia?

This edition published 2022

Published by Library For All Ltd
Email: info@libraryforall.org
URL: libraryforall.org

Where Is Liberia?
O'Leary, Nancy
ISBN: 978-1-922835-26-0
SKU02719

Where Is Liberia?

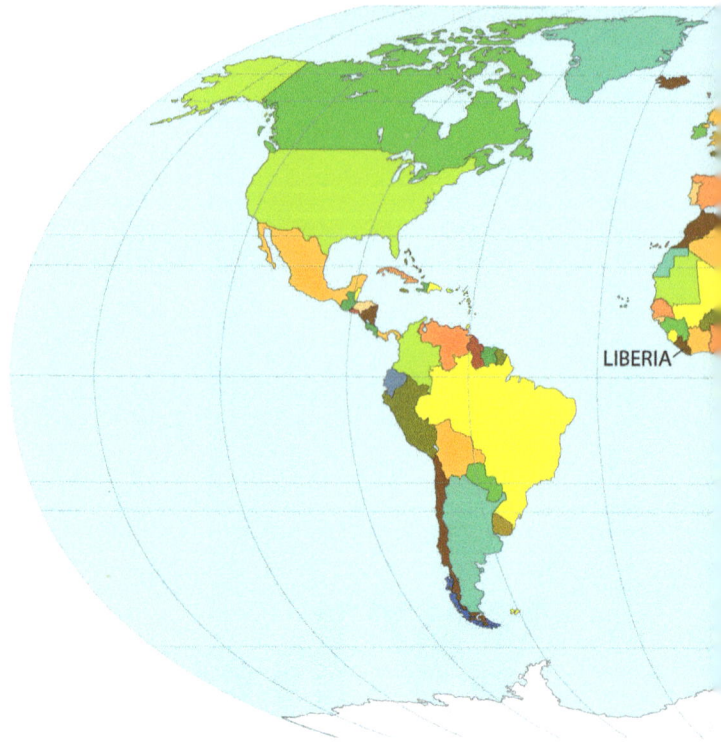

LIBERIA

This is a map of the world.
It shows all of the countries.
There are almost two hundred
countries in the world. Liberia
looks very small on this map.
Can you find Liberia?

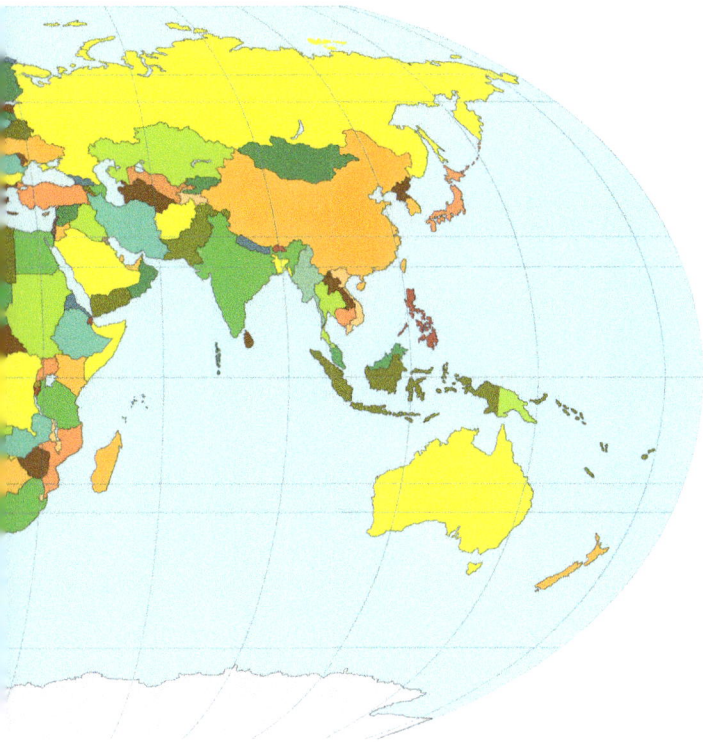

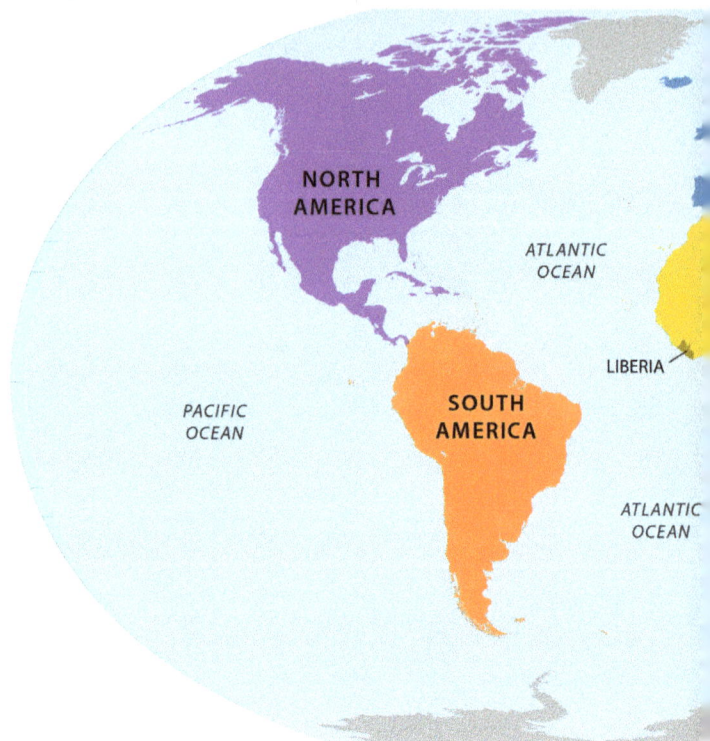

NORTH
AMERICA

ATLANTIC
OCEAN

LIBERIA

PACIFIC
OCEAN

SOUTH
AMERICA

ATLANTIC
OCEAN

ARCTIC OCEAN

EUROPE

ASIA

PACIFIC
OCEAN

A

INDIAN
OCEAN

AUSTRALIA

ANTARCTICA

This map shows the continents of the world. A continent is a large piece of land. Africa is one of seven continents. Africa is big. The map also shows the oceans. Can you find Liberia on this map?

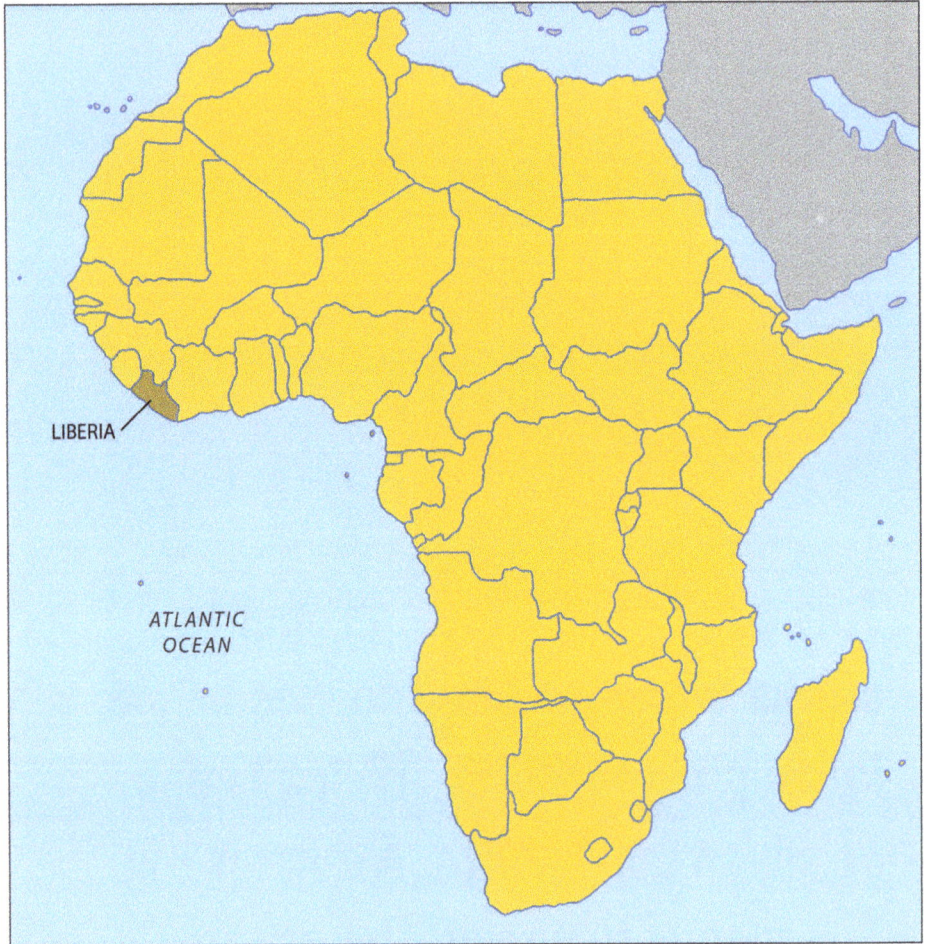

LIBERIA

ATLANTIC
OCEAN

This map shows the continent
of Africa. Africa has more
than fifty countries.
Can you find Liberia on this map?

Liberia is on the west coast of Africa. This map shows Liberia and the countries around it.

GUINEA

SIERRA
LEONE

LIBERIA

CÔTE
D'IVOIRE

ATLANTIC
OCEAN

SIERRA
LEONE

GUINEA

Voinjama

Tubmanburg

Bopolu

Sanniquellie

CÔTE
D'IVOIRE

Gbarnga

Robertsport

Kakata

Bensonville

Zwedru

Monrovia

LIBERIA

Buchanan

River Cess

ATLANTIC
OCEAN

Fish Town

Greenville

Barclayville

MAP KEY

• city

Harper

This is a map of Liberia. This map has a key. A key tells what things on the map mean. The black circles on the map are cities. How many cities does this map show?

This map shows the land and water of Liberia. The key shows the rivers and mountain ranges.

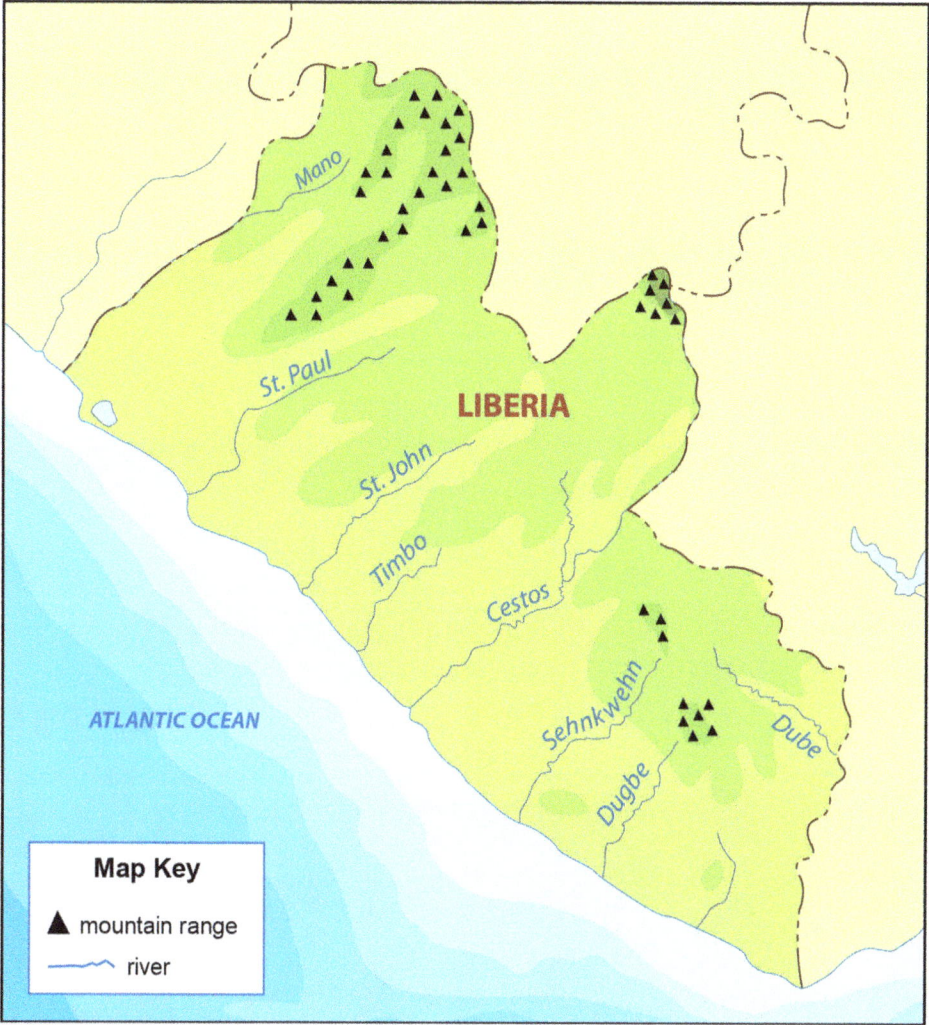

Map Key

▲ mountain range

〜 river

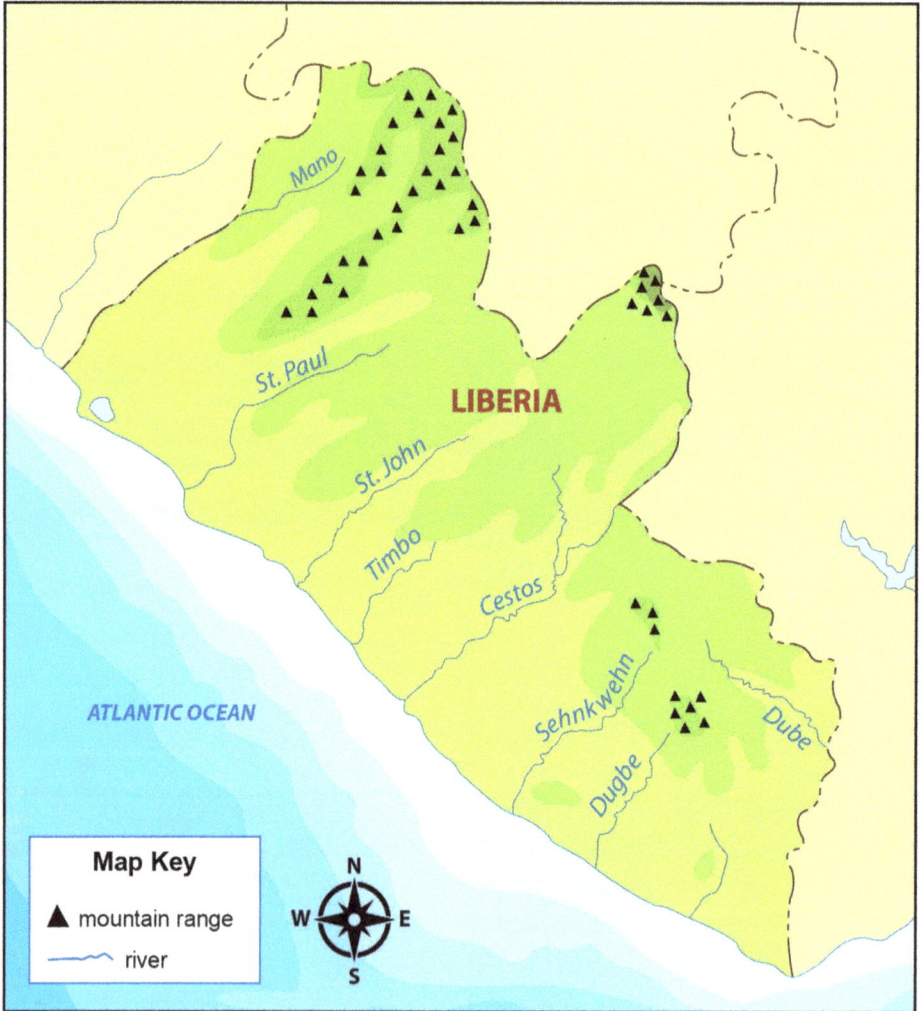

Map Key

▲ mountain range

～ river

N W E S

LIBERIA

Mano

St. Paul

St. John

Timbo

Cestos

Sehnkwehn

Dugbe

Dube

ATLANTIC OCEAN

This map of Liberia has a compass.
A compass shows the directions
North, South, East, and West.
A compass can help you find your
way from one place to another.

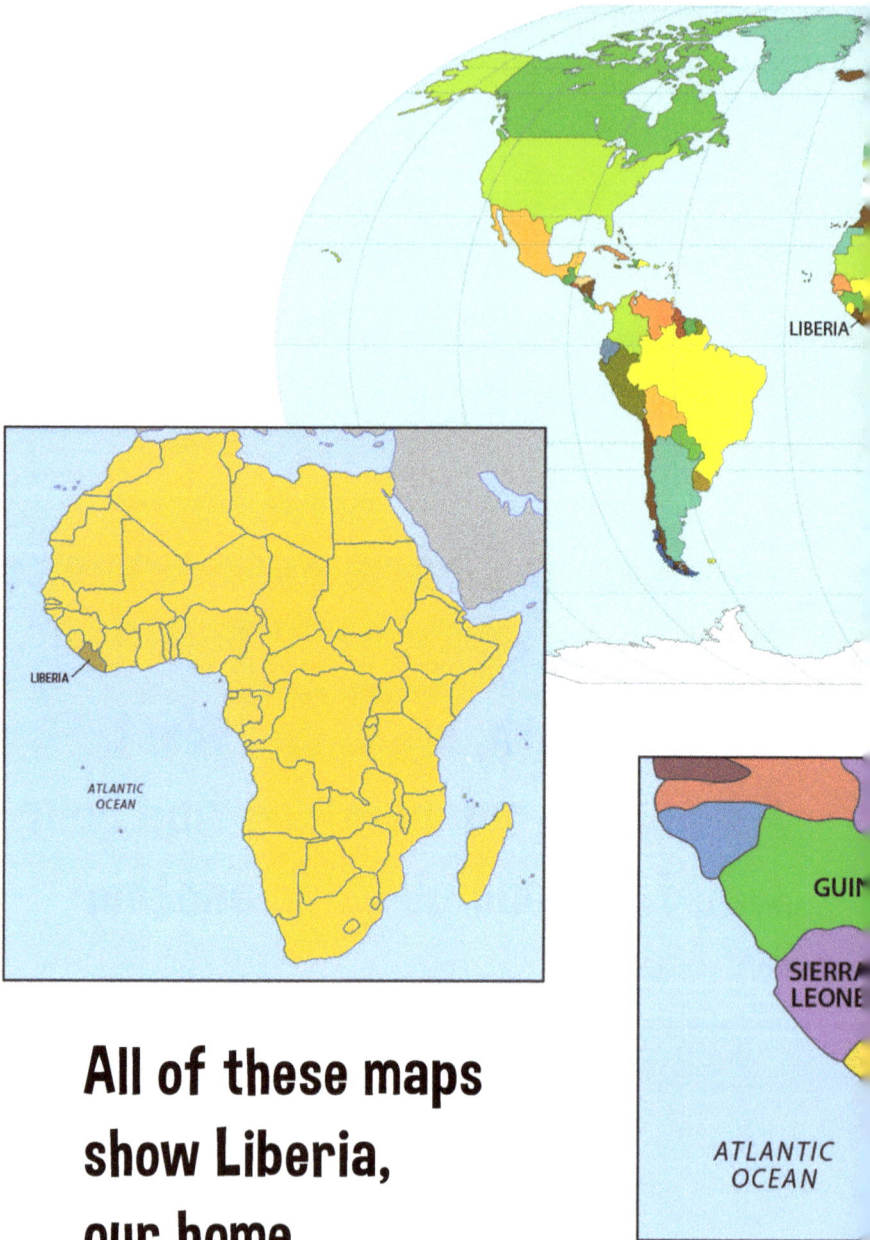

LIBERIA

LIBERIA

ATLANTIC
OCEAN

GUIN

SIERRA
LEONE

ATLANTIC
OCEAN

All of these maps
show Liberia,
our home.

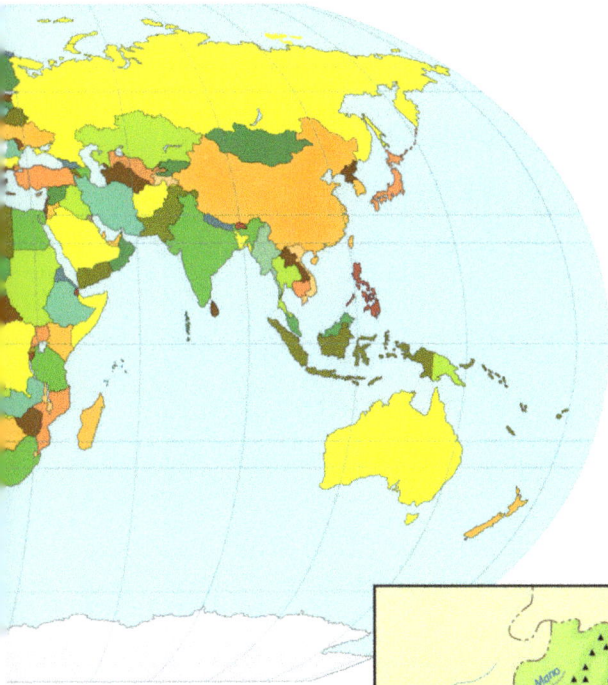

CÔTE
D'IVOIRE

Mano

St. Paul

St. John

Tiemba

Cestos

Sehnkwehn

Dugbe

Dube

LIBERIA

ATLANTIC OCEAN

Map Key

▲ mountain range

~ river

You can use these questions to talk about this book with your family, friends and teachers.

What did you learn from this book?

Describe this book in one word. Funny? Scary? Colourful? Interesting?

How did this book make you feel when you finished reading it?

What was your favourite part of this book?

download our reader app
getlibraryforall.org

About the contributors

Library For All works with authors and illustrators from around the world to develop diverse, relevant, high quality stories for young readers. Visit libraryforall.org for the latest news on writers' workshop events, submission guidelines and other creative opportunities.

Did you enjoy this book?

We have hundreds more expertly curated original stories to choose from.

We work in partnership with authors, educators, cultural advisors, governments and NGOs to bring the joy of reading to children everywhere.

Did you know?

We create global impact in these fields by embracing the United Nations Sustainable Development Goals.

9 7 8 1 9 2 2 8 3 5 2 6 0